My Path to Math

123456789

MEASUREMENT

Penny Dowdy

Crabtree Publishing Company

www.crabtreebooks.com

Author: Penny Dowdy
Coordinating editor: Chester Fisher
Series editor: Jessica Cohn
Editors: Reagan Miller, Molly Aloian
Proofreader: Crystal Sikkens
Project coordinator: Robert Walker
Production coordinator: Margaret Amy Salter
Prepress technician: Margaret Amy Salter
Logo design: Samantha Crabtree
Cover design: Harleen Mehta (Q2AMEDIA)
Design: Tarang Saggar (Q2AMEDIA)
Project manager: Santosh Vasudevan (Q2AMEDIA)
Art direction: Rahul Dhiman (Q2AMEDIA)
Photo research: Anju Pathak (Q2AMEDIA)

Photographs:
Alamy: Peter Bowater: p. 15; Image Source Black: cover
Bigstockphoto: Karl Martin: p. 11 (right)
Corbis: Owen Franken: p. 9
Dreamstime: Mk74: p. 6 (middle); Reno12: p. 14; Svetaphoto: p. 7
Getty Images: Image Source: p. 13
Istockphoto: Joachim Angeltun: p. 8 (left); Matjaz Boncina: p. 11 (left);
    Johanna Goodyear: p. 10 (right); Stepan Popov: p. 8 (right), 23;
    Nina Shannon: p. 10 (left); Sami Suni: p. 17
Jupiter Images: p. 1, 19; Image Source: p. 5
Shutterstock: Amfoto: p. 12; Robert Asento: p. 21 (bottom);
    Jacek Chabraszewski: p. 6 (right); Eric Gevaert: p. 18 (right);
    Mau Horng: p. 21 (middle); Morgan Lane Photography: p. 18 (left);
    PhotoCreate: p. 4; pzAxe: p. 16; Brad Sauter: p. 21 (top); Elena
    Schweitzer: p. 6 (left); Stillfx: p. 8 (middle)

Library and Archives Canada Cataloguing in Publication

Dowdy, Penny
    Measurement / Penny Dowdy.

(My path to math)
Includes index.
ISBN 978-0-7787-4341-5 (bound).--ISBN 978-0-7787-4359-0 (pbk.)

    1. Measurement--Juvenile literature. I. Title. II. Series: Dowdy, Penny.
My path to math.

QA465.D69 2008   j516'.15   C2008-906086-5

Library of Congress Cataloging-in-Publication Data

Dowdy, Penny.
    Measurement / Penny Dowdy.
      p. cm. -- (My path to math)
    Includes index.
    ISBN-13: 978-0-7787-4359-0 (pbk. : alk. paper)
    ISBN-10: 0-7787-4359-4 (pbk. : alk. paper)
    ISBN-13: 978-0-7787-4341-5 (reinforced library binding : alk. paper)
    ISBN-10: 0-7787-4341-1 (reinforced library binding : alk. paper)
    1. Measurement--Juvenile literature. I. Title. II. Series.

    QA465.D75 2008
    530.8--dc22
                                              2008040149

Crabtree Publishing Company

www.crabtreebooks.com   1-800-387-7650

Published in Canada
Crabtree Publishing
616 Welland Ave.
St. Catharines, Ontario
L2M 5V6

Published in the United States
Crabtree Publishing
PMB16A
350 Fifth Ave., Suite 3308
New York, NY 10118

Published in the United Kingdom
Crabtree Publishing
White Cross Mills
High Town, Lancaster
LA1 4XS

Published in Australia
Crabtree Publishing
386 Mt. Alexander Rd.
Ascot Vale (Melbourne)
VIC 3032

Contents

Measure Me!

My doctor measures my **height**.
I can find the **length** of my foot.
I can see the **width** of my hand.

My teacher can measure how far
I run. There are many ways to
measure me!

Activity Box

What words tell how long something is?
List some of the words.

My height is a measure
of how tall I am.

5

Ways to Measure

You can measure with numbers. You can also measure by showing people or things together.

There are silly ways to measure, too. You can measure with shoes. You can put shoes end to end. You can see how many shoes long you are.

Who is shorter of the two?

Measuring Tools

You can measure with tools. A **ruler** measures by inches and feet. A **meter stick** measures by meters. A **centimeter ruler** measures by centimeters. Meter sticks and centimeter rulers are called **metric tools**.

Yardsticks are longer than rulers. I can measure my bed with a yardstick. **Tape measures** are even longer. I can measure a room with a tape measure.

Activity Box

A ruler is one foot long. The foot was named for the size of the king of England's foot.

Rulers measure length.

What is Mass?

Sometimes I want to know if something is heavy. Something heavy has more **mass** than something light.

Look at the butter and the refrigerator on the next page. You know which is heavier. The refrigerator is heavier. It has more mass.

Activity Box

Mass is not about size. This balloon is about the same size as the rock. Are their masses the same or different?

The butter is light. The refrigerator is heavy.

Tools For Mass

A tool called a **scale** measures mass. When I stand on a scale, it shows a number. That number is my mass.

A **balance** also measures mass. A balance is like a seesaw. One side holds weights. The other side holds the thing to weigh. I add weights to the balance. Once the two sides are even, I know the mass!

This boy is finding the mass of a block using a balance.

13

What is Capacity?

The kitchen is filled with measuring tools. A cup holds things like water or milk. It holds a certain amount.

The amount something holds is its **capacity**. Imagine two friends each getting a glass of juice. The glass that holds more juice has more capacity.

Everyone wants the glass with greater capacity!

See For Yourself

Jars and glasses are not always the same size. They are not always the same shape.

Compare these bottles. Which bottle has more capacity?

Activity Box

The bottles are not the same size or shape. Why is it hard to see which has more?

These jars are easy to compare.
They are the same size.

Measuring Capacity

One way to measure capacity is by using **measuring cups**. There are lines on the side of a measuring cup to show the amount inside the cup.

There are other tools for measuring capacity, too. People in the United States measure capacity using tools such as teaspoons, cups, and **gallons**. In other parts of the world, people measure capacity using metric tools.

The capacity of this milk jug is one gallon.

You can line up the liquid with the marks on the measuring cup.

I Can Measure!

I can measure. You can, too.
What tools show how long or
tall something is?

What do you have to measure
mass at home? How do you find
out how much you weigh?

What do you have to measure
capacity at home? When do
you need to measure capacity?

Activity Box

Ask an adult to help you use
measuring tools at home.

The ruler and measuring tape measure length.

The scale measures mass.

Glossary

balance A measuring tool used to find mass

capacity The amount an object holds

centimeter ruler A short measuring tool used to find metric length

compare To show one thing against another for measure

gallon A large measure of capacity

height How tall or high an object is

length How long an object is

mass How heavy an object is

measuring cup A measuring tool used to find capacity

meter stick A long measuring tool used to find metric length

metric tool A tool for measuring

ruler A short measuring tool used to find length in inches

scale A measuring tool used to find mass

tape measure A very long measuring tool used to find length

width How far across an object is

yardstick A long measuring tool used to find length in feet

Index

Printed in the U.S.A. — CG